Bearables

• ◆ •

Parables of Bear Wisdom
for Everyday Living

JANE AND MIMI NOLAND

DRAWINGS BY MIMI NOLAND

HarperCollins*Publishers*

HarperCollins*Publishers*
77–85 Fulham Palace Road,
Hammersmith, London W6 8JB

A Paperback Original 1995
1 3 5 7 9 8 6 4 2

Copyright © Hazelden Publishing 1993
Drawings by Mimi Noland

The Authors assert the moral right to
be identified as the authors of this work

A catalogue record for this book
is available from the British Library

ISBN 0 00 638462 5

Printed in Great Britain
by Scotprint Ltd, Musselburgh

This book is dedicated to bears everywhere,
who are finding it harder and harder to just be
bears in increasingly threatened habitats.

The Bear-Human Connection

Humans have a longstanding affinity for bears, maybe because bears, like humans, are built to be upright, at least part of the time. Because bears can stand up and look us in the eye, we tend to humanize them—pretend that they think our thoughts and talk our language.

A young bear, fuzzy and vulnerable, has an almost mystical appeal for us, while the unpredictable power of an adult bear fills us with awe and trepidation. We dream about bears, good dreams and bad. We tell stories about bears (some turn into myths). We see bears in stars. We make bears into totems. We make bears into toys.

Especially since the introduction of the teddy bear in 1902, inspired by President Theodore Roosevelt's bear cub, we have glossed over the true bearness of bears and made huggable facsimiles to give to our children—and ourselves. These little interpretations of bears, covered in plush or velveteen and filled with straw or cotton or foam, have a wonderful variety of winsome shapes and expressions. They have come to represent comfort and companionship. Sometimes a stuffed bear is called upon to temper a child's sadness or even to help fill a void of human love.

As for real bears, we have a respectful fear of them when our trails cross theirs. We admire them for being flexible and, generally, for minding their own business.

The small stories in *Bearables* are based on actual bear behaviors and true bear-human encounters. Bears in the drawings demonstrate how their woodsy wisdom translates into practical human situations.

When it comes down to essential life-lessons, we can learn a lot about what we need to know just by watching bears.

"Ask now the beasts, and they shall teach thee."

Job 12 7:7

Introducing (from a Discreet Distance) the Goodbears

Serena and Dunbar are good bears who are always trying to be better bears. They are excellent citizens of the northern forest, living quietly by bear codes, usually bothering no one except an occasional settlement of ants or bees, a mouse, or a lazy crayfish. In fact, they are so fine and upstanding, and so predictably bear-like, that they have become known as the Goodbears.

Serena Goodbear is a wise mother, who has parented eight off-spring in her cub-bearing years: a single male, Bjorn, now far away in another territory, eating up a storm, no doubt, and bal-looning into a creature to be reckoned with; two females and a male named Flora, Fauna, and Fedora, respectively (also known as the rainbow triplets because each is a different color); and two sets of male/female twins. The older twins, born two-and-a-half years ago, are Kuma and Ursula. The younger pair, in their first summer of exploring and learning, are Dubu and Serendipity. Dubu is "bear" in Swahili and Serendipity (Dipity for conve-nience) borrows from Serena's own name.

The father of Dubu and Dipity, Dunbar Goodbear, is usually off somewhere foraging. He comes around every once in a while to slap the ground (as some bears do) and put in his two cents as a role model.

Let the Goodbears who lumber, slumber, and romp through these pages show you how bearables—examples of bear wis-dom—can become parables for humans to live by.

Waking Up Joyful

In early spring, Serena unrolled her large body and came out of hiding, along with the ferns (they were doing the same thing) and the snowdrops. Dubu and Dipity emerged behind her from the dark of their birth den. They squinted at the light, at sunbeams leaning on trees and laying bright paths on the forest floor.

Instinctively, the cubs knew that a first order of business—after they got used to the luxury of space—was to play. Play would tone them up and make them strong. Before long, they were rolling around, delighting in their twinness and their gymnastic talent. They lifted their muzzles to the sights and smells of a whole new, damp, and wonderful world.

Dubu and Dipity didn't have to be taught about joy—or about how to show it either. They knew.

Celebrate mornings.

Make play a priority.

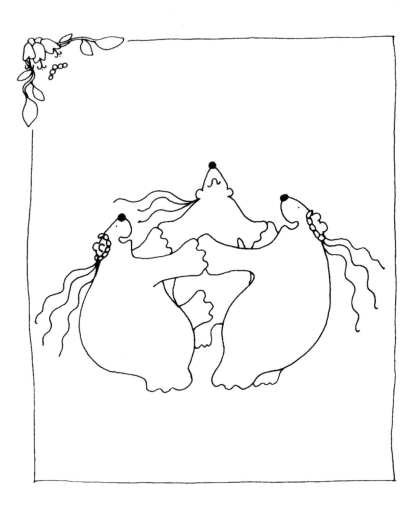

Celebrate mornings.

Make play a priority.

About Acceptance

(or Bad Things Happen to Good Bears)

Dubu and Dipity were tumbling around, wrestling, within earshot of Serena, when the thimbleberry bushes parted to frame a monstrous, eyeless face. It was so misshapen, full of lumps and welts and asymmetries, that it could not possibly belong to the family Ursidae.

The cubs scurried toward Serena, who had risen up on her back legs and was peering at the intruding monster. They waited for her cough, their signal to scramble up a tree.

Instead, she said (in bear snuffles), "Kuma, is that you?"

And so it was. Their older brother, Kuma, on the prowl for a honeycomb in the brilliant light of noon, had been attacked by a cloud of irritable bees. Serena, who had seen plenty of beestung bears in her time, nudged Kuma toward the river bank for some healing mud.

Wobbling her head (as some bears do), Serena passed along a truism that bears have known since the trees in the forest primeval were blossom-high to a buttercup.

Bees happen.

Bees happen.

Playing It Safe

Like all of Serena's cubs before them, Dipity and Dubu had been taught an immediate response to possible harm. At the first crackle or whiff of danger, Serena would cough, and the cubs would shoot up the nearest tree before you could say "Airstream." There they would stay, with only the glint of their little eyes showing through the leaves or the pine needles, until Serena signaled an "all clear." They had practiced and practiced their routine through dozens of intrusions like these, lesser and more serious:

A forester's jeep and the roar of a buzz-saw.

A disagreeable male bear.

A gusty wind, sending snapped-off branches crashing to the forest floor.

A wolf—no, a Golden Retriever leading a family of two-legged hikers.

A bull moose.

Even a klutzy rabbit, noisier than most.

While hanging out in treetops (as young bears do), Dubu and Dipity already had assimilated an important lesson:

When you're up a tree, ask yourself why.

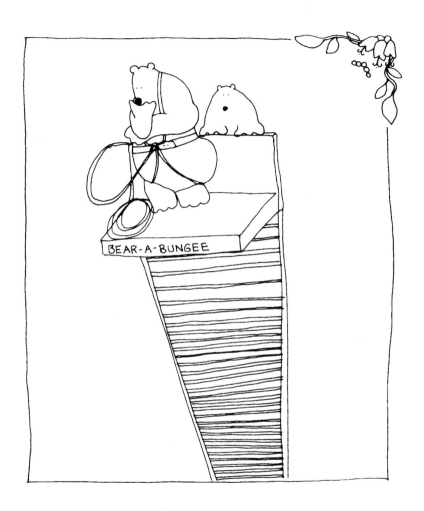

When you're up a tree, ask yourself why.

Havens and Hiding Places

One afternoon in early autumn, Aunt Arctica was hobnobbing with Serena (as mother bears do) while Dubu and Serendipity and their cousins hunted, mostly in vain, for a few late-ripening raspberries. They paused at an unfamiliar sound. It was alternately high and low—a cross between the bwahnk-bwahnk of a Canadian goose and the burble of the river after a rainstorm.

"Ahem," coughed both mothers at once.

Aunt Arctica's cubs disappeared effectively into the rusty foliage of an oak.

But Dubu and Dipity made a poor choice. The nearest tree was a young willow, so slim they could hardly hug it or get their claws into it. The chill of the season already had turned the foliage into hanging chains of gold.

Clinging to opposite sides of the skinny tree, the two cubs set up a pendulum motion, back and forth, bending the tree first one way, then the other—like carved figures on an old German clock! The ride might have been fun, if they hadn't been trying so hard to vanish.

That was far from the result. Their dark bodies, set off by the gold branches shimmering around them, were unmistakable baby-bear shapes. Two humans on the trail (for the sound they had heard was human laughter) pointed up at them, still laughing.

They laughed, that is, until they caught sight of Serena baring her teeth (as bears do) and took off like a couple of white-tails. Truth was, the humans' disappearing act was a lot more successful than the cubs.'

Make sure your havens are solid—and huggable.

If you want to be anonymous, blend in.

Make sure your havens are solid—and huggable

If you want to be anonymous, blend in.

A Big Bear's Small World

Serena had scooped out a spot at the base of a white pine so her cubs could "shade up" on a hot summer day while she went foraging (not far). Dubu and Dipity watched her from their nest.

They saw their big mama bear pick up a gull feather delicately in her huge front paws and turn it over and over like a love letter. With the same delicacy and precision, they saw her overturn a log and put a paw over an ant hill, then lick the ants from the paw one by one with relish. They saw her snap up a grasshopper in mid-hop, and nip the red thimbleberries from a bush, leaving nary a berry.

Although she was large-scale enough, standing upright, to view the grand sweep of her surroundings, she seemed to zero in more on a Lilliputian world—on plants and creatures a trillionth (or so) of her own size. Nothing, from a grub to a currant, was too tiny to capture her beady-eyed attention.

Any bear knows you can make a perfectly adequate meal out of hors d'oeuvres (2,001 acorns, for instance), especially if you eat all the time and never turn down even the most inconsequential tidbit on summer's platter.

Don't overlook the little things.

Don't overlook the little things.

Out on a Limb

Dubu, trying to learn everything at once about being a bear, was inclined to be a bumbler. Once, on the edge of the river, he pawed at a feeble fish, only to have it come to life and thwap him in the nose. In trying to scoop up an ant colony in a fallen tree, he moved so slowly that most of the ants escaped, scuttling into a bear-raid shelter under the log.

One day, after one of Serena's danger drills, he tried to back down a northern pine and got himself hung up. There he sat, straddling a branch and swinging his little legs frantically. With one cub in the tree and one on the ground (Dipity had descended with considerably more grace), Serena fussed.

Only with the most desperate maneuverings did Dubu manage to work himself free and get down—claws slipping, collecting slivers as he went. He landed in a humble heap at Serena's feet.

With no rear-view mirrors and a short neck, a bear learns fast:

Back down gracefully

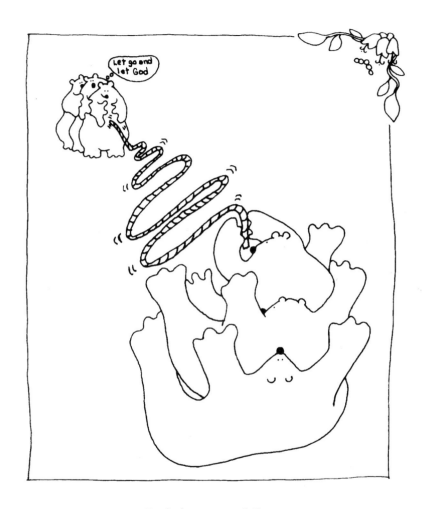

Back down gracefully.

Tracks and Tracking

As Serena steered her youngest offspring to the river bank to look for bugs and perhaps a frog, she pointed with her nose to a gallery of animal tracks in the mud—pawprints of raccoons, hoofprints of deer and moose, the slither mark of a snake's belly, rabbit tracks followed by the fresher prints of a fox.

There they all were, as clear as the handprints of stars cast in the cement forecourt at Mann's Chinese Theater on Hollywood Boulevard.

Serena led the cubs through tufts of swamp grass, making their presence at the river harder to detect.

The lesson was plain:

**Keep your feet clean,
and nobody will come after you.**

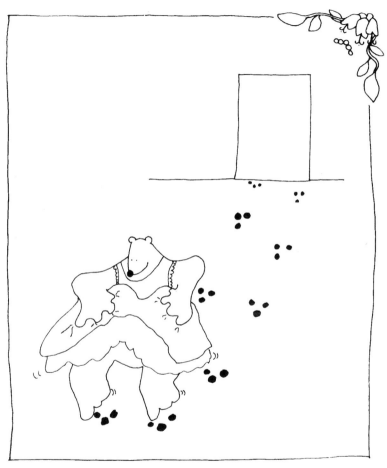

Keep your feet clean, and nobody will come after you.
(Or tiptoe, and they'll think you're a stork.)

Learning to Make Do

The season was dry. Berries were sparse. Mice and beetles seemed to be more woods-wise and elusive than usual. Unusually brave as mother bears go, Serena huffed (the equivalent of a sigh of resignation) and led her twins down the side of a gravel road, past dusty raspberry bushes, to the town dump. Poking around, they found gastronomic treasures—cans lined with the remnants of tomatoes and creamed corn, barbecued ribs picked not quite clean, mushy bananas in their skins. Dubu was especially sharp-nosed at rummaging in the dump. He turned up part of a cherry pie, a package of pancake mix, and (treat of treats!) a plastic bottle half full of syrup.

Dining at the dump had its drawbacks. It was a less exclusive cafeteria than a berry patch. Other bears (mostly adult males oozing self-confidence) lumbered in. Sometimes at dusk people in vans would come to gawk, with their children all squeaking and carrying on ("Lookit, Mom—that HUMENDOUS bear is smiling at me!"). Serena, never far from a tree, kept a warning "ahem" ready in her throat at all times.

Still, in a lean year for berries, the dump was an alternative. And most bears—the Goodbears included—were cautious opportunists.

When nature fails to provide, seek alternatives.

When nature fails to provide, seek alternatives.

The Cost of Being a Nuisance

Serena, in her ursine wisdom, steered Dubu and Dipity away from behavior that could get a bear in trouble.

They'd heard about one of Aunt Arctica's older cubs, a character named Oso, who had made himself into a nuisance bear. To his detriment, he discovered easy street—in a summer colony of humans bordering the big lake.

He earned notoriety as a discriminating burglar when he hooked two New York strip steaks, thawing on a cabin deck, and left the chuck roast behind.

Then, with unbearlike boldness, he marched into a cabin where two teenage humans were baking M & M cookies and helped himself to a whole batch, still warm, while the cooks went out through the bathroom window.

In another clear case of breaking and entering (through a slit screen), he opened the freezer compartment atop a refrigerator and pulled out everything but the ice cubes. Again, he was picky. He turned up his nose at three packages of Lean Cuisine (the cabin owners found them later on the floor, dismantled but uneaten) and made off, instead, with a loaf of raisin rye and a carton of Haagen Dazs.

Not even the peppery grandmother who pelted him with pears and epithets ("Bad bear!" "You thief, you!" "Go on, GIT!") convinced him to abandon his brassy ways. Always Johnny on the spot when food was involved, Oso had arrived just in time to help her unload her grocery bags.

The final test of human patience came when Oso sneaked into the colony's dining lodge before a Sunday brunch. After dipping messily into the sugar bowls on the tables, he was discovered sitting on the bun warmer, warming *his* buns and trying to roll up the lid to get at the Danish.

Oso was never seen in the forest again. His relatives liked to think that he was picked up and moved to a new area, away from temptation, where there were no soft-touch humans or lodges with bun warmers.

If life seems too easy, worry.

Do not covet your neighbor's buns.

If life seems too easy, worry.

Do not covet your neighbor's buns.

The Rumored Ferocity of Mothers

During Dubu and Dipity's first summer, Serena was huffily over-protective. Standing on her back feet, head up, ears back, mouth open, she appeared to challenge all who ventured near her youngest.

One afternoon, as they were stuffing themselves in the raspberry patch, Serena drew herself up to her tallest and fiercest and woofed. Hers was a regular storybook bear woof, guaranteed to scatter humankind. Dubu and Dipity stood up too, to get a better sniff and a clearer look.

All they could see were two very small humans, about their own size, who turned and fled, swinging their little buckets, spilling raspberries as they ran. Hardly a threat—unless, of course, the small humans had fierce mothers standing by too. Serena took no chances.

Dubu and Dipity thought all this maternal huffing and woofing was making a beaver lodge out of an ant hill.

**Mothers often protect you fiercely,
even when you don't need it.**

Mothers will protect you fiercely, even when you don't need it.

Obedience (or Else)

To make sure her wishes were taken seriously, Serena counted on a sequence of controlling behaviors.

If Dubu and Dipity pretended not to listen when she called, she would first whine a little, then huff. If they still ignored her, she would stand up and flatten her ears, show her teeth, and look tough. If that didn't work either, she would pick up a big paw and cuff the little rebels into attention. She saved this last technique mostly for emergencies that demanded quick action.

As for those outside her immediate family—any humans or stray adolescent bears or other sizable animals that happened by—they never stayed around to test Serena past her first huff.

Huff before you bluff.
Bluff before you cuff.
And cuff (gently) only as a last resort.

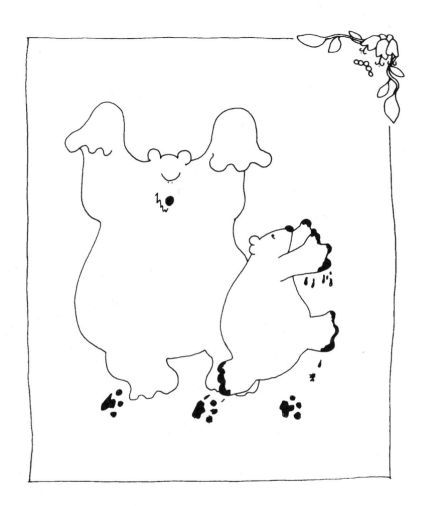

Bluff before you cuff.

Ancestors

Of course, Serena Goodbear did not have a long view of history. She didn't know about the Miacid, a little tree-climber who lived 25 million years ago and is said to be the many-times-over granddaddy of bears, as well as of wolves, coyotes, foxes, dogs, and raccoons. She'd never heard of the Etruscan bear, considered an ancestor of brown and black bears. She was not aware of the land bridge that became a bear trail across the Bering (Bearing) Straits hundreds of thousands of years ago. Nor did she know about her far-flung cousins in seven other bear species (if you count the giant panda). Although she did not *know* all this consciously, she carried the memories in her genetic make-up.

Serena was content to keep to her spot on earth, a marked off, four-square-mile territory of forest and meadow.

She did remember her mother, Superior, at whose knee she had learned most of what she knew about getting along on civilization's edge—from highways to hazelnuts. She even learned to sniff out the difference between humans with guns and humans with harmonicas (some bears like the sound). Serena honored her mother—and the whole history of beardom—by passing on these coping skills to her own cubs.

Honor your forebears.

Honor your forebears.

Rainbow Bears

Two of Serena's triplets, daughters now in their fourth summer, came around now and then. They still hung out together part of the time. And when they did, they were almost certain to be tailed by at least one or two pushy humans with cameras. For they were not your run-of-the-mill black bears. Flora was the color of a ripe acorn, and Fauna was gold as a honeycomb. Fedora, the male, now off on his own somewhere, was reddish, like a maple leaf in late October. Serena herself was more brown than black, with the usual lighter muzzle.

These three cubs became especially good climbers, because Serena had practically worn out her warning cough during their first summer. She was always having to get them up and out of the way of the pesky paparazzi.

Once, four years ago, Serena heard a suspicious click and dispatched her rainbow triplets up a tree. A photographer happened to be up there too, seeking the perfect vantage (as photographers do). The cubs clambered over him, shredding his shirt and peeling his pockets. Then they sat on the branches over his head and stared down at him with their shiny little eyes.

If Serena was aware of this human presence, she ignored it (as some bears do—to avoid trouble). She never once looked up. The tree party became a secret shared by the triplets and the quivering cameraman. Eventually, the cubs backed down, raking him again!

The photographer stayed cramped in the tree until the bears wandered off. Then he took off at a crashing clip for his Land Rover—and the iodine in his First Aid kit.

To Dubu and Dipity, who were acquainted with their rainbow siblings, a bear of a different color was no big deal.

To avoid trouble, turn your back on it.

Brothers and sisters come in all colors.

To avoid trouble, turn your back on it.

Brothers and sisters come in all colors.

A Spicy Variety of Temperaments

Serena, as her name indicates, was known for being unflappable, for seldom acting in haste. Most of her daughters took after her, except acorn-colored Flora, who was inclined to be a flirt and a little silly, and Dipity, who was hyper. (She was also lucky; she found the juiciest June beetle larvae and the most dandelions.) Although Dunbar was plenty imposing and sometimes impatient, he was a pussycat as male bears go.

Fedora, the reddish male, had mood swings. He had been known to carry an unbearlike grudge. (Beware of getting into HIS acorns!) As for Kuma, a run of bad luck had toughened him up—bees and wolves and a human who hurled a skillet at him with the competitive vigor of an Olympic athlete. Although he wasn't mean, he was wary. The youngest, Dubu, was a clown. He played it up for all it was worth, jesting his way into the hearts of Serena and everyone else who happened to catch his act.

Humans, in their passion for organizing data, are apt to think everybody in a certain species acts alike. Bears know better.

Don't settle for stereotypes.

Don't settle for stereotypes.

The Swap

One afternoon, Aunt Arctica dropped by with her cubs. As if by prior arrangement with Serena, she nosed Dubu and Dipity to her side along with her own little ones and led all four down a new trail to a dessert of chokecherries. Serena then vanished for some well-deserved R and R—the ursine equivalent of lunch and a matinee on her own.

Dubu and Dipity didn't seem worried, even when Serena, on her return, left them again with Aunt Arctica and borrowed *her* two (their young cousins) and sashayed off for a gourmet dining tour in a different direction.

In three or four hours, the cub shuffle was over. Both mothers and all cubs had sorted themselves into their respective families of origin. The outing had expanded the young ones' horizons, as well as their palates. For their part, the two mothers seemed unusually free-gaited and good-humored, as if sharing responsibilities—even temporarily—had lightened their burden of conscientious motherhood.

For perspective, trade offspring now and then.

For perspective, trade offspring now and then.

The Great Honey Hunt

Bears are known honey-lovers, as any beekeeper in bear country knows. With few beekeepers around, Serena taught Dubu and Dipity how to sniff out honeycombs at the meadow's edge.

Dipity and Dubu had distinctive styles of honey-hunting. Dubu liked the challenge of bees in trees. He would plan carefully, staking out the colony, eyeballing its potential, weighing the risks. He prepared himself for the ascent like a well-outfitted mountain-climber about to take on Kilimanjaro.

Dipity sniffed out her bee bunch on the ground. By the time Dubu had drawn his blueprints for Operation Bees-in-the-Treetop, Dipity, sticky from nose to toe, was sitting, her back against a pine, happily consuming a honeycomb. (After all that planning, Dubu's bees turned out to be hornets, which he ate out of disappointment.)

Serena shared in the honey's sweetness. She deserved it. It was her Teacher of the Year award.

The sweetest honey is not always in the tallest tree.

The sweetest honey is not always in the tallest tree.

Learning the Territory

Serena spent endless summer hours showing her cubs around her territory. She knew it well—every trail, every spongy spot underfoot, every fallen tree, every cluster of berry bushes.

Serena knew the clearings where humans camped and which trails the bull moose took down to the lake for a drink. She knew where the thickest clover and peavine grew and where the tallest oak trees stood. And she knew how to get back home, no matter how far she meandered.

Dubu and Dipity tagged along. When she peered, they peered too. When she stopped to sniff, they stopped to sniff too, memorizing as they went. They would come back to these same haunts as adolescents, as sure as if they'd been equipped with maps.

With all the sniffing and peering and learning, the cubs were on sensory overload. By the time Serena had wound up her lab course in geography, Dipity and Dubu would know the territory and its boundaries like the backs of their paws.

Know your boundaries.

Know your boundaries

Denning Up

In October, as the ground hardened and the foliage crispened, Serena and her cubs got yawny. Food was harder to find. Dustings of snow announced that heaps of snow would not be long in coming. And bears, with all that weight (they eat nonstop all summer) and their shortish legs, do not plow through snow-drifts with ease.

It was time to den up, to poke around for a winter hideout. Dubu and Dipity thought Serena might lead them back to their birth den, but she was in the mood for something new (as mother bears are). This was not surprising—anyone who'd been stuck for months in an efficiency with squirmy newborn twins, in pretty much the same position and with the same old decor, certainly could use a change!

The three of them explored promising brush heaps and gaps under rock ledges. They finally settled for the hollow base of a fallen tree, behind a protective fence of roots. Serena, as a senior mom, got first dibs on the good dens. (Her older cubs would have to work up to the choice ones.)

Dipity and Dubu helped her line it with moss and grass and ever-green branches—all gathered within fifty-or-so feet of the den. Dipity strayed just a few feet farther and discovered an old shag bathmat on a low-sagging clothesline behind a cabin. Since the humans who summered there had closed up the place for the season, Dipity took her own sweet time in removing the rug. She unhung it rather deftly, leaving the clothespins. Then, with youthful pride, she dragged it to the den, where Serena made a mattress of it.

Already punchy, they crawled in to doze away the short days and long nights of the northern winter.

Express yourself through your den decor; prowl for "found art."

Take long naps.

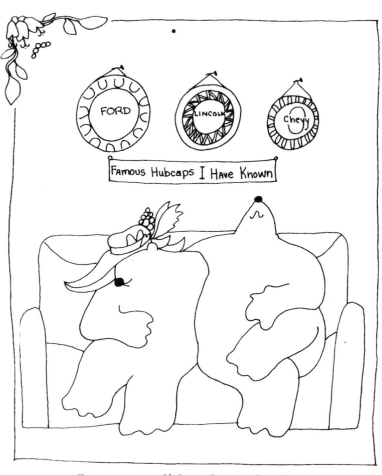

Express yourself through your den decor;
prowl for for "found art."

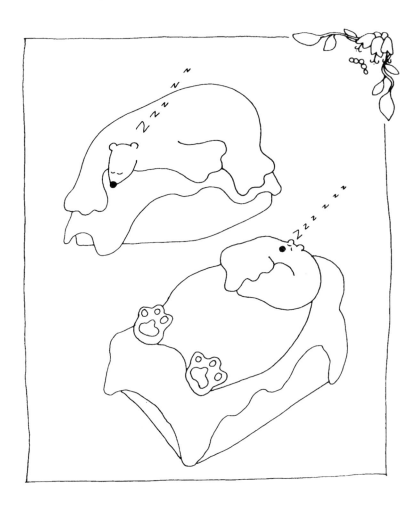

Take long naps

A Time for Introspection

Denning up gives northern bears like the Goodbears an advantage over some other animals—especially humans, whose headlong pace seldom allows for a breather. Denned up bears are not out cold—like bats or woodchucks or other true hibernators. Bears just cool off slightly, slow down, and sleep. Some even come out once in a while for a groggy look around.

In winter, bears have time for introspection, time to digest the summer's experiences—along with those thousands of nuts and berries and bugs that have turned them into logy butterballs.

Maybe Serena and her cubs dream about finding abandoned picnic hampers filled with S'mores, or roaming new territories thick with mountain ash. Or maybe they have grandiose athletic dreams—about flagpole-sitting, or scaling the tallest and most elderly white pine, or zipping along a trail at 35 m.p.h.

Take time to reflect.

Take time to reflect.

A Lesson in Quietude

In spite of their bulk, the Goodbears made sure that their goings and comings were strictly hush-hush. They glided through the forest silent as fish. Humans in Serena's territory report that they seldom hear the rustle of brush or the crack of a twig under a bear foot, or the sound of ursine cursing at some unbearable frustration.

A quiet human on a trail can catch a glimpse of a shadow that *might* be a bear slipping out of sight behind a tree. A noisy human probably won't see that shadow at all and will remain innocently unaware of being in bear country.

One thing is sure: in wintertime the Goodbears practice being even quieter than usual—which is spooky quiet at *any* time of year. Their talent for silence keeps Serena and her cubs safe. Moose and deer browse beside their den in winter. Except in the rarest circumstances, even wolves pass bears by.

When scientists intrude briefly on a sleeping bear family to check on their habits and health, the intrusion no doubt becomes a bear-dream—and the bears go right back to being quiet.

Learn the value of being quiet.

Learn the value of being quiet.

Hanging Around Home

Dubu and Dipity (as cubs do) would spend their first birthday and a second winter with Serena—maybe (although rarely) even a third winter, if food was hard to come by, or if she hadn't kicked them out in favor of her biennial summertime fling and another pregnancy.

For bear sows, motherhood is a God-given responsibility and a full-time job. No lick-and-a-promise parenting for Serena! Starting with helpless, blind babies no bigger than squirrels, she hovered over them until they grew into capable, three-quarter-size bears. Serena kept her cubs around until she was sure they had a basic education in the three C 's: climbing (to vamoose up a tree), clawing (to turn up food), and calendars (to plan ahead for the exigencies of each season). With this careful upbringing, they would have a good chance of getting through the trials of adolescence and making it on their own.

Serena's older offspring checked in occasionally too. When it came time to stake out territories of their own, they would confer with Serena about whether to homestead in a new place or to stick around their cubhood haunts and sublease some of her real estate.

Give yourself time to grow up.

Give yourself time to grow up.

A New Perspective

Dubu and Dipity's second April rolled around. The two partly grown cubs and Serena, still punchy, left their winter den behind.

This time, the young ones had a whole lot more savoir faire. Their surroundings were not so overwhelmingly new. Both noticed that, compared with last summer, the trees seemed smaller, the lower branches more reachable. Serena herself seemed to have shrunk some. The giant trillium wasn't giant anymore. While digging for wild onions took much less time and effort, peering down for a close-up of a miniature bellflower seemed to require deep knee bends.

The river was narrower and less turbulent, the pond smaller, the trails shorter. All in all, their world was a more manageable place.

A few more winters and they would learn, as Serena had learned:

Nothing changes much—except your perception.

Nothing changes much—except your perception.

Risk and Reality

Dipity, in spite of her youth and her small size, was fascinated by fish. So was her father, Dunbar. This was somewhat contrary to the habits of their species (*Ursus americanus*), who generally were not big on fishing. But the river that fell into the great lake at the edge of Serena's territory was too compelling to ignore. Now and then, Dipity had a chance to pick up pointers, as she watched Dunbar from afar, pinning and nabbing suckers like a real pro.

One afternoon Dunbar stood downstream from her, where the river deepened past the rapids. He was a handsome sight, his dark fur glistening with spray from the falls. He exuded the arrogance of a fisherbear who really knew what he was up to! In fact, his skill would have inspired even his Alaskan cousin, considered the best in the business.

Other bears recognized that Dunbar claimed rights to this spot, and they, wisely, hung back. All but Dipity. Wading out for a better look, she slipped on a rock, lost her grip, and began bobbing and careening on the whitewater that swept her toward the huge bear.

He could have mistaken her for a beaver and pounced on her. But he was so startled by the thrashing furball in HIS fishpond that he merely stood up and popped his jaws (as some bears do).

His daughter scrambled to the bank, shaking-wet and a little smarter about hydrokinetics and her own limitations.

It's okay to set goals beyond what's expected of your species.

Before you risk, get realistic.

It's okay to set goals beyond what's
expected of your species.

Before you risk, get realistic.

Survival of the Flexible

Serena Goodbear was the soul of flexibility, bearing out an ancient bear mandate: *Do what it takes to adapt to whatever place or predicament you find yourself in.*

If a forest doesn't meet your needs, try a meadow. If skunk cabbages are scarce, go after catkins. If berries are scanty, load up on nuts. If the he-bear you fancy isn't available, find another. If you don't have cubs of your own, borrow some.

If you live in a shady place, wear your black coat; if home is an open, sunny slope, deck yourself out in cinnamon or beige so you won't overheat. And, as long as humans are around, learn to put up with them, even when they are bothers and bores—and when they fail to respect boundaries (including their own).

Because they're compromisers, bears, eons after colonizing North America, still manage to roll with the punches and land on their feet (in spite of such unnatural disasters as the British coronation of 1953, for which 700 black bears became hats for the Royal Guards).

Above all, be adaptable.

Above all, be adaptable.

Saving the Natural World

The Goodbears are masters at saving energy—stoking up on food in summer, and in winter cutting out travel, turning down the temperature, and confining themselves to small, easily heated domiciles. They also try to space themselves out, so that no single territory will be depleted of edibles by too much grubbing and picking.

Most Goodbears do their best to save their environment—especially trees. They've learned that a shortsighted bear can fell a thin tree, just by leaning on it for quick backscratch. In keeping with this philosophy, Serena taught all her young ones to be conservation-minded. (She would not be proud of some of her western relatives who—taking their cues from humans—sacrifice longterm prosperity for immediate gratification. These ruinous bruins in the State of Washington have been known to debark—and kill—Douglas firs so they can munch on the cambium layer. Now, even these greedy cousins are learning to eat other things.)

Carefully, Serena pointed out which flowers to eat and which to avoid. With heroic self-restraint, she passed over a certain kind of blossom in the spring, giving the plants a chance to produce something tastier later: BLUEBERRIES.

Respect your environment.

Respect your environment.

Moon-Dipping

Dipity, now a dreamy adolescent old enough to ignore cubhood curfews, liked the night. She also liked water, sloshing around quietly in ponds and rivers and the edges of the big lake.

One midsummer night when a full moon shone, she left Serena and Dubu rummaging in a clearing and waded into a calm place where the river spread into a pond. Tonight it was smooth as a mirror. In its surface, she could see her own shadow. She could also see the reflection of a perfectly round moon. There it was, shimmering, silver as a fish, a perfect disc to hold between her paws. She batted at it, attempting to dip it up, first with one front paw, then the other. Of course, the circle broke into smithereens of light, only to form again when she stood up and stopped ruffling the water.

Dipity stayed there, trying to dip up the moon, until the reflection passed out of the pond. Then she gave up and went to find Serena and Dubu. She would try again on some other glassy-calm night with a perfect moon.

Serena did not scold. The Goodbears honor independence, even when it involves such adolescent folly as moon-dipping.

Reach for the moon—wherever you find it.

Reach for the moon—wherever you find it.

Jane Thomas Noland is a writer, humorist, and books editor. She is the co-author of the classic meditation book *A Day at a Time* (now with a million copies in print); author of *Laugh It Off*, a book about the importance of humor and laughter in losing weight, also illustrated by her daughter, Mimi Noland; and co-author, with award-winning illustrator Ed Fischer, of the best-selling gift book *What's So Funny about Getting Old?* With high school counselor Dennis Nelson, she also wrote a Twelve Step guide for teenagers, *Young Winners' Way.* She is a Phi Beta Kappa graduate of Smith College and a former feature writer for the Minneapolis Star-Tribune. She and her husband, Richard, parents of two grown children, live in Wayzata, Minnesota.

Mimi Noland illustrated Kathleen Keating's *The Hug Therapy Book* and *Hug Therapy 2* (bears) and *The Love Therapy Book* (dragons). The two hug books together have sold more than 700,000 copies and have appeared in over twenty foreign editions. She is the author-illustrator of *The Hug Therapy Book of Birthdays and Anniversaries* and of *I Never Saw the Sun Rise* (written at age fifteen under the pen name Joan Donlan). Her illustrations appear in another best seller, *An Elephant in the Living Room,* by Jill Hastings, Ph.D., and Marion Typpo, Ph.D.

Mimi Noland, a Skidmore College graduate in psychology with further training in police work and animal science, is also a singer and songwriter. She owns and operates a horse farm in Maple Plain, Minnesota.

Mimi Noland